'In My Mind's Eye'

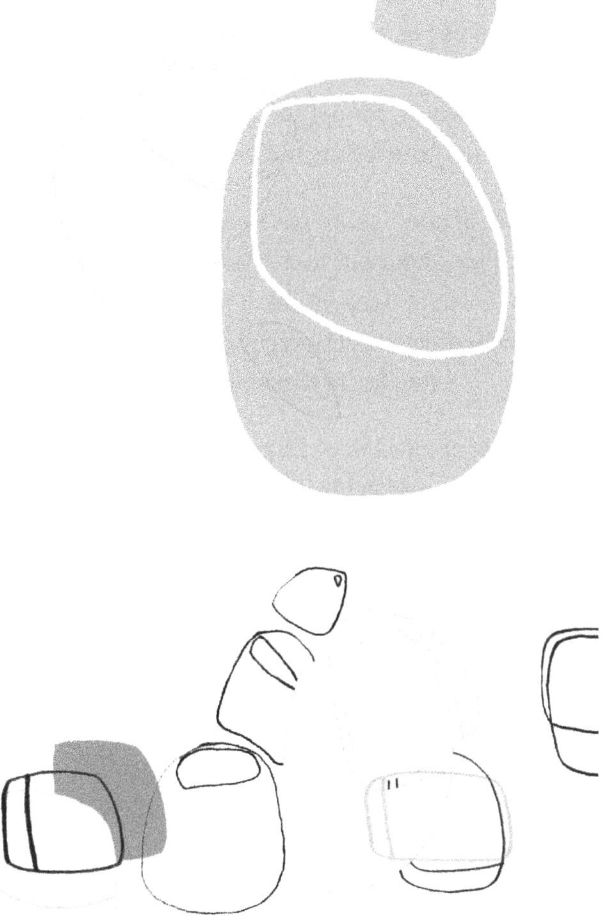

MJ.STEVENS

'IN MY MIND'S EYE'

For me words are so fascinating, anytime I write a new story, a poem or even a song...it all begins with words! Knowing the right things to say and write are very important to me, so by researching as much as I can in regards to certain words, for me the best part is putting it all together on paper and letting my imagination run wild.

Writing these set of poems sure gave me a lot of pleasure, most of them I had to really think about but then there were others that just seem to come from somewhere deep inside of me and writing them were easy. I like this way of writing it's very exciting and leaves one with a sense of stability in knowing ones talent.

As for this book of poems I have given each chapter a different feel, using themes from my life and in life in general. From my day's of growing up on the streets of North West London to my relationships with women, my family and how I see my life in this world.

So I hope that you enjoy 'In My Mind's Eye'

MJ Stevens

CONTENTS

Street Life

Moments

Life

Human

Love

mjs
music

‘Street Life’

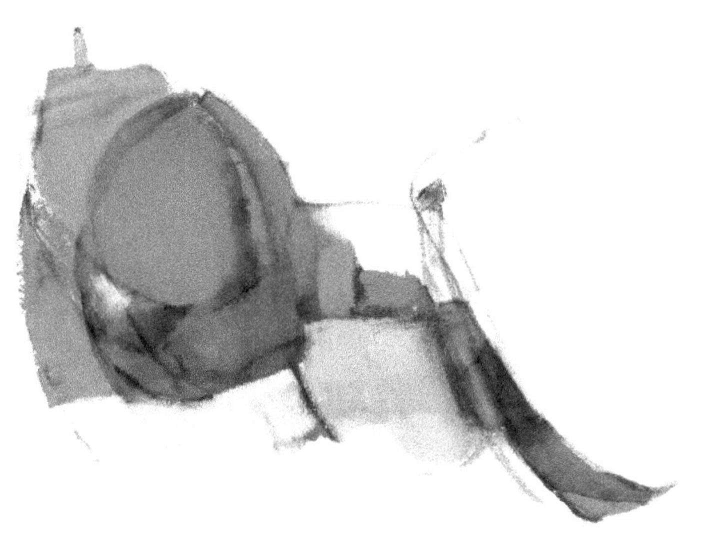

'Street Life Rules'

She's hot, he's not
They are cool, she's a fool!
Dress to impress,
Street life rules!

Nike this, Adidas that
Armani suits,
Gucci boots!
Black or white,
Street life rules!

London, Paris
New York, Rome
Everyone is a media clone!

Orange, Virgin
T-mobile, 02
Cyberspace
Emails and Viruses too

The Rich, the Poor
The Homeless the True...
Tell me who believes in you...?

Street Life Rules
Will dictate
Just who you are
So don't relate.

'Are You like Me'

Are you like me?
Were you born into a world of poverty?
Did your family have money?
Did you live in a big house?
Or are you from the projects?

Are you like me?
What school did you go to?
Did we share the same class I bet you fly upper class?
Yes I went to school
In fact I did very well
How did you do?

Are you like me?
Are you from a one parent family?
Do you have a father?
I wish I knew mine
How many brothers and sisters do you have?
Is your family close?

Are you like me?
Have you ever been racially abused?
Have you ever been stopped in the street and searched by the police?
Have you ever been called a fucking nigger by someone from a foreign country?

Are you like me?
Do you own a gun?
I sure don't
But here I lie
Waiting to die
As you all watch me on your TV
So are you like me?

'Ebony'

Hide and seek
Only you can make me see
History...
Token words won't leave me be...

Now was it real?
I missed the chance to set you free...
Chemistry...
Don't let me be another dream

Is this Humanity?
Is this my destiny?
This is Ebony...

Lonely in this world
Breathe the air and you will learn...
Energy...
There's a place for you and me...

Is this Humanity?
Is this my destiny?
This is me I am Ebony...

'Kicking and Screaming'

Kicking and screaming
Punching and biting
Slapping and spitting
Cursing and shouting

Smoking and bitching
Fighting and stealing
Fingering and posing
Bullying and raging

Football and swearing
Trainers and sweating
Teachers and students
Begging and lying

Boys and girls
Kissing and crying
Under age sex
Truth and denying

Exams and tests
Scores and failure
These are the things
That I remember

School and college
Work and money
Looking back in anger
Isn't life funny?

'Candy Man'

On every avenue
On every street
You will find the candy man.
He comes in all shape and sizes
Could be a woman he could be a man
What he sells makes some of us well

The rich and the poor
Uses him more
The police try their best to control the flow
But between you and me they won't win the war

Hour after hour the people want more
So the candy man grows, adapts and controls
Factions will crumble and the heavens will roar
But the candy man will be the last man standing
Happy to sell you more!

'Urban Thoughts'

To fly is to be free
To make love is to feel need
To cry is to open your soul
To scream is to let one know

To hurt is to feel pain
To cheat is to make gain
To kiss is to know bliss
To touch is to say, I wish

To try is to compete
To read is to know speech
To learn is to gain knowledge
To have respect is sure
One big challenge

To die is a natural thing
To pull a trigger these days means nothing
To be a racist is nothing new
To abuse makes you a fool

To preach is sometimes divine
To write can be a crime
To take is always foolish
To stand for what is right make's people notice

To be black can be hard
To be white is a charm
To know love in your heart
Now that's where it all starts

King of Kings

Black is black
Where's all my people at!
Jay Z, Left Eye Lopez
Snoop Doggy Dog
50 Cent and T.I
Hip hop rules the world
The people love the words
Rapping is cool
RnB is no fool
Just ask J.T
It made him so much money
Michael Jackson beware
The prince of pop
Stole your flair

Will Smith
Doesn't need to swear
For he is righteous
And makes us care
King of the white screen
He may be
But DMX still makes us scream
Run DMC
I watched as a teen
Biggie Smalls
I wanted to be
Tupac was a shining light
But hip hop made him sour
What a great actor he would have been
But the demons inside did him in

King of kings
They all my be
But for me one man made me believe
That anything is possible
And his name is Mohammad Ali

'Colour, Racism, Creed'

When I am out and about
I see many things
When I walk the streets
I can see the heat
Women in short skirts
Girls with pleats
Sexy females
High heels and sneaks

To look is ok
Even better when you say
'You look great, you look fine'
But I always hesitate
Any response is good
A wink or a smile
But always say it to her eyes
Be she black or be she white
A woman worth is definitely worth while
But lately for me
I just can't seem to understand
The woman in the street
Or maybe it's just me?

Colour, Racism, Creed
All the above dictates for me
For I see that choice matters most
So liking someone
Is mostly false
Hoping love finds you
One night stands
Won't really help you
Understanding what being human is
Look beyond the skin
And faith will guide you

So when I am out and about
And when I walk the streets
I hope that when we meet
You won't judge me before I speak
For I am Human
Just a man Indeed...

‘Moments’

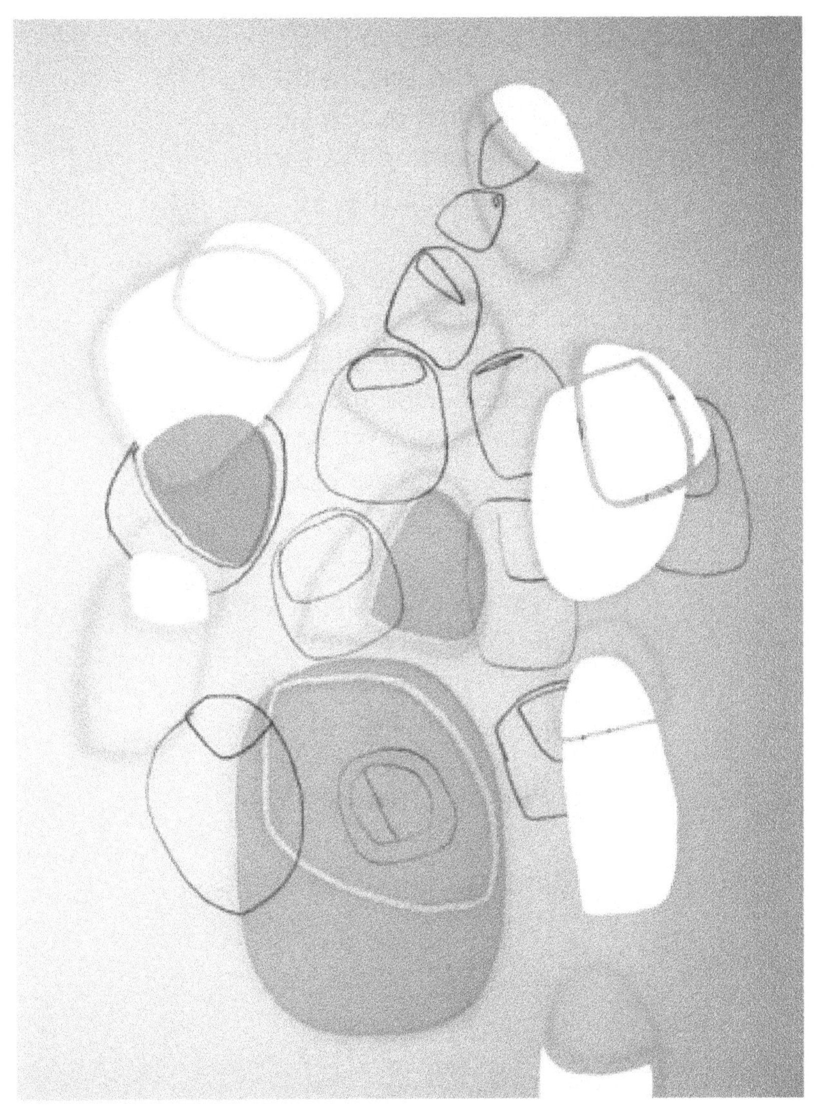

'Don't make no Sound'

What can I say?
What can I do?
Mid day sun tell me the truth!
Pushed to the side
And turning the screw
Is that the best that you can do?

Movers and Shakers
They know what to do
The dreamer's decide just when to move
Don't push me away
Don't turn the screw
I must confess
I love what you do!

Take a piece somehow
But don't break the rules
Turn it around
But don't make No sound!
Is this justice now!
When you play the fool?
Turn it around
But don't make No sound!
Don't make No sound!

'Green Pastures'

Taken aback by love,
Make's you wonder more about trust.
These days not even a kiss,
Can save you from lust.

When you want something you can't have!
Do your best to forget it!
Move on to green pastures!
Never look back to those disasters!

Hiding your feelings is never a good thing!
Just look at me, I nearly lost everything!
Only words from a child like mind!
Made me realize that I was blind!

So I wish you well in all your endeavours!
And remember that time is a friend that always delivers!
Being in love is never easy!
But falling in love is still a great feeling!

'If Only'

Search for forgiveness and make amends!
Break free from the chains that bound you there!
Only in my world do you belong!
Say a little prayer but make it strong!
Who wants to live forever?
I want to stay forever young!

Pure and innocent that's what you are!
Patent energy will get you far!
Only in my world do you belong!
Open up your heart that's never wrong!
Who wants to live forever?
Who wants to stay forever young?

If only we did!
If only we tried!
If only we could!
I'd turn back Time!
And realize and make you mine!
You'd say my name!
There'll be no pain!
No need to cry!
If only we did!
If only we tried!
If only we could!
If only we could!

'I've been around'

There's an honest good vibration here!
It comes from all the good things you say!
I know in time I'll lose my patience!
This is just something I do!
If only you could see my nation!
My people live with dignity!
Can't you see the situation?
So please governments around the world!
Change your policies!

See these feelings endlessly!
We will make this history!
I'm living for my fate!
Walking around I'll find my way!
That's the one thing I can say!
Don't you think the same?

I've been around and I've been down!
Yes I have been around but still I seem to fall down!

'Jealousy from Within'

Even with friendship we die a little!
When someone you care for believes not the truth!
You then believe that you are not true!
But just remember who you are and that those battles are there to be won!
So never give into the jealousy from within!

People will come and people will go!
But just as long as the water flows but watch out when you're heading for!
The waterfall!
Because we seek what we believe to be goodness!
But when goodness becomes deceitful then that's when,
you must define the jealousy from within!
And only then will you know where you stand!
So you've made your choice & now you must live with it!
You can't change the past but only in time can you change just how you feel!
So never give in to the jealousy from within!

'Leaving'

There's a road that I call saviour!
There's a street that I call Grief!
And in these desperate times I wonder!
What will it take to make you see!
That I'm leaving...leaving this street!

When words mean nothing!
When minds begin to change!
And shattered dreams cometh everyday!
What will it take to make you understand!
That I'm leaving...leaving you today!

You shout, you scream and you rant!
You fail, you break and you run!
But above it all the sky remains blue!
Now it's time for you to understand!
That I'm leaving...leaving you anew!

'They think they know me'

They think they know me!
They think I Lie!
They think indifferent!
So they become allies!
She makes up stories!
She makes up crimes!
All of this just to make me cry!

The two become one!
But one is two!
There must be others!
That believe what they do!

Infatuation makes her feel!
Deception keeps it real!
Although I sit and wonder!
Will the both of them ever see!
Just what they did!
Just what they have done!
Did I deserve the hate they've shown?

All I wanted was to love!
All I wanted was to feel!
Is it so bad to want something real?
Now they talk with patted breath!
Just because I never said!
What I truly am is just for me!
At least I know my destiny!

So now I sit and watch things be!
They continue to die within me!
If the child is truly me!
Then why deny what should be?

'Understand'

A Little Boy...
Dying On the Street!
A Mother's Tears...
Making Waves on TV!
A Soldier with a Gun in His Hands!
Here I Am...Trying To Understand!

Some People...
When Driving In Their Cars!
With Violence...They Become Men at Arms!
But When She Smiles!
My Whole World Is Good!
But Deep Down Can It Be So True?

Lover's Pride...
Take My Greed Tonight!
I Am Here It Is Time to Fight!
Just Hold On And Let This Fear Disappear!
So Don't You Cry...I Will Be Your Guide!

Take My Hand and I Will Be Your Man!
Lay This Seed and It Will Grow So Deep!
Turn Around...There Will Be No Sound!
So Broken Wings!
Learn To Fly Again!
...Understand?

'True Blue'

When you blink,
You can miss so much!
When you sleep,
The world continues!
And you miss even more!
When you are awake,
Life goes fast!
Sometimes slow,
When you watch!
That's when you hear,
Then everything becomes clear!

When you dance,
You set yourself free!
Emotions are bright,
That's when you'll be!
Anything you want,
And have anything you need!
When you hold a woman,
Close to you!
Feel her heartbeat!
Feel her heat!
And when she responds,
Tell her what you feel!

When you try,
That's when you fly!
Fear exist,
But never say die!
Jump into life,
Let life jump into you!
And only then,
You'll see true blue!

'Music'

Subtle sounds that oozes through!
Feel the emotions in that tune!
Rapping beats that make you jump!
Dancing grooves makes you pump!

Solo guitars earn their way!
Keyboard melodies make you stay!
A jazzy riff can undo!
Any anger that flows through you!

Blues is cool!
Rock is hard!
Metal is deaf!
Pop is mild!

Soundtracks are great!
Sometimes not!
Takes a good movie!
To make us watch!

But when it all comes together!
The music shines!
Individual magic!
Is what's left behind!

Music is live!
Music is life!
When a band plays well!
Everything is right!

'Rain'

No more aces left to play!
No more lines upon my face!
There's goes another day!
There's nothing more to say!
They told me it's ok!
But still they walked away!
No words, no touch, no pain!
I guess it was the rain!
It must have been the rain!

I watched you fall apart!
You never were that smart!
These dreams you had for me!
They live with misery!
You told me it's ok!
But still you walked away!
More words, more touch, more pain!
I guess it must have been the rain!
It must have been the rain!

So this is how the story goes!
Live your dreams and don't let go!
Everyone's the same!
Don't keep asking questions why!
This is when you live or die!
Just look into my eyes!

No more aces left to play!
No more lines upon my face!
There goes another day!
There's nothing more to say!
They told me it's ok!
But still they walked away!
No words, no touch, no pain!
I guess it was the rain!
It must have been the rain!

'Simple Man'

Here...Here in my heart!
No where to start!
No where to hide!
Soon...Soon it will be!
Oh! Can't you see?
I am in need!

Free to be, who I am!
Come take my hand!
And stand with me!
Do...Do what you can!
You must understand!
Just what you are!

Simple Man!
Don't you run away!
Keep your head held high!
Don't you ever stray!
This Simple Man!
With these eye's so bright!
Don't you fade away!
Don't you ever stray!

'Change'

He sometimes breaks!
He sometimes delays!
Feels alright!
Because those were the days!

He watched the sun!
And the rains dictate!
Bye and bye!
They all disappeared!

She takes so long!
To pick up the phone!
Turns inside!
Because now is the time!

To sacrifice everything!
That she owns!
Bye and bye!
She knows when to cry!

It's only change!
It's only what remains!
It's only change, change, change!

'One'

One had brown eyes!
One had green eyes!
Another had blue eyes!
And one had black eyes!

One had a great mind!
One had a great body!
One was pure!
And the other was demure!

One was sexy!
One was wild!
One was beautiful!
And one was all mine's!

One had long hair!
One had short hair!
One was blond!
Brunette was the other!

One always smiled!
One always cried!
One was tough!
And one was just too much!

One was wise!
One always sighed!
One loved to be kissed!
One loved to take the piss!

Each one said they loved me!
Each one never lied to me!
And still to this day!
Each one still thinks of me!

‘Life’

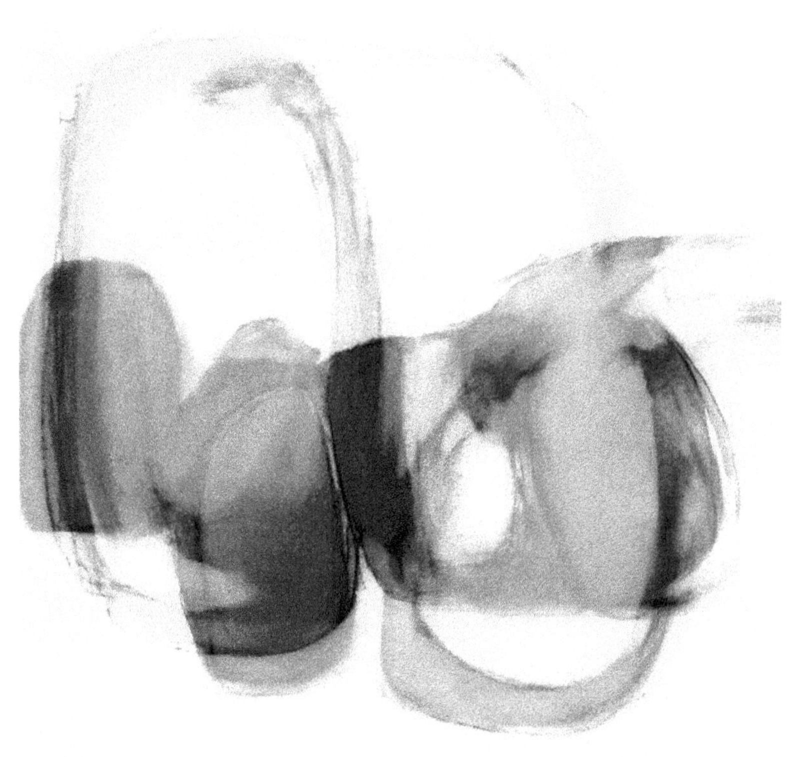

'Another Day'

Something said, can only be!
Whatever we want it to be!
Something said, can only make you feel pain!
Or feel great!
Something said, is either right or wrong,
but something said, is all you know!

It's another day...Enjoy it...Treasure it!
Because not every day is the same!
Some days are good;
some are bad!
But rarely are the same!

It's for us to find that piece of buried treasure in each day!
And keep it close to our hearts - Forever!
And then remember it some other day!

Reason why?
Well! In every soul we all want to feel!
But in our mind's eye the dream is never, never real!
So live each day for you, live each day for real!
And remember
Life was made for you, to go out and steal.

'Dance the Night Away'

I don't know the reasons why?
Tainted lies and day's gone by!
Screaming loud like voices in a crowd!
What do you think of me right now?

She said, 'To dance the night away'
Sail along, don't dream of
Yesterday...she said,
To dance the night away!
And heavens knows...I danced
The night away!

Born to lose!
Still nothing less will do!
Take my life...I watched until it died!
In this season I lived a thousand times!
So tell me what do you think of me right now?

She said, 'just dance the night away'
Sail along, don't dream of
Yesterday...And she said,
To dance the night away!
And heavens knows,
We danced the night away!

'Friends'

Like sand in a glass!
Friend's will seep through!
Like the minutes that go by!
A friend you will lose!
Keep in mind that when in time!
A friend in need is a friend indeed!
The beginning is always fine!
Just like love it will leave you blind!
But a friend can be wonderful until!
They find a clink in your armour!
That will leave you wondering!
Where to draw the line!

What is a true friend?
A true friend knows the right thing's to say!
A true friend hold's you dear no matter what you say!
A good friend stand's for what is right!
When it comes to your affairs!
A good friend is the one!
Who tells you when to stair clear!
I had friends once!
Well I thought they were!
But when it came to the crunch!
Friendship became a blur!
Taking sides is easy!
But when you forget reason!
You end up bleeding!

So true friendship what does it mean?
Heaven to some but not for me!
My friends came and went just like a dream!
Now I stand here disillusioned to the extreme!

'Looking At Art'

Looking at Art is sometimes like
Waking up Drowsy,
Dull, Tired & Useless!

Looking at Art can be like,
Waking up with a beautiful woman!
Sweet, sure and simply wonderful

Looking at Art is mostly like,
Watching paint dry!
Boring, Pointless and Tasteless!

Looking at Art is like,
A Subtitled French Movie!
Misunderstood, sexy and dark!

Looking at Art for me is like,
Playing the music that I love!
Brilliant, Excellent and Timeless!

Looking at Art I guess can be,
Whatever you want it to be!
But Looking at Art is just,
Looking!

'Money'

Money I don't have and money I never will!
Although I work very hard!
Money leave's me ill!
Time and time again I earn!
Time and time again I learn!
That money comes and goes!
And money always flows!
Money is real and money is wrong!
Still I pay for it!
Just like you all!
Time and time again I fall!
Time and time again I Know!
That when the buck stops!
There's nowhere to go!
Money is good, money is fun!
Is that the drink talking?
Must mean I am drunk!
Time and time again I watch!
And time and time again I shop!
Still the money in my pocket!
Leave's me down and broke!

'Sex in the City'

'What women want' is the question on everybody's lips
What to wear...
When to leave...
Buying shoes that just don't fit!
Look good in jeans,
Look good in skirts!
Maybe suits or slacks!
Like a temptress on a movie screen!
That you just can't have!

We got Sex in the City!
What a pity...Don't it make you mad?
Women going crazy, Men Likewise!
Don't get left behind!
Sex in the City!
What a pity, she drives me wild!
Women going crazy, the Men Likewise!
Don't get left behind!

She's got style, she's got grace!
Now I'm lost without a trace!
Armani this, Gucci that!
Sweet money makes it pay!
She look's good in jeans!
She look's good in skirts!
Sometimes suits and slacks!
And Like a Beauty Queen on a movie screen!
That you can never, ever have!

'The Difference'

This is amazing,
This is so strange!
Colours by numbers,
People in chains!
But I do know the way they feel today!
Do you know this feeling?
Do you know this pain?
Rapped up emotions in my head!
Can you see the difference in just what they say?

This is my moment!
This is my chance!
To find direction!
And make some sense!
We've been torn apart!
And told that they just don't care!

So you may be heaven!
You may be truth!
But this rhyme and reason!
Will see us through!
This is amazing!
This is so strange!
Rapped up emotions in my head!
But I can see the difference in the words that they say!
Now I can see the difference in just what you say!

'The Nightmare'

It's Cold, and it's dark!
Then Rain Starts To Fall!
Somewhere between Hell & Heavens Fall!

Distant Voices Trails behind Me!
Apparitions Appear Before Me!
Why Here? Why Now?
What does this mean?
I Feel Alive, I Feel Weak!
My Heart Beats In Time!
My Mind Says, Die!

Who's there? Oh! Fuck This Nightmare!
Got To Wake Up!
This Is Not Real!
Who Is That Behind The Steering Wheel?

Leave Me Alone I Cry!
But Still I'm Alive!
Do What You Must!
Do What You Will!
Just Leave Me in Peace!
I Beg Of You!

Still! There's No Sound!
'What Do You Want'
Why Fuck With Me?
I am Nothing...Can't You See!
Then Silence Breaks...Hear Me Fall!
I am Dead...Never More!

'TV COPS'

Sipowitz, Colombo, Kojak, Poirot,
Starskey and Hutch, Morse and Frost...
All great TV cops...
Oh! How we love to watch them solved crimes.
Even when they get hurt we don't want them to die...
Isn't it amazing how we love our TV cops...?
But as you know in real life cops suck...
Most are racist's pigs that couldn't solve a fuck!
All they do is stop us blacks and call us niggers behind our backs...
Isn't it funny how we love our TV cops!
The cop's I know only think they know,
That to intimidate with force!
Make's them strong!
But all they do is make us know that to trust a cop is the worse crime known.
So why do we love our TV cops
Because it's alright for Huggy Bear to snitched for Hutch!
It was cool when Kojak sucked his lollipop
And when Andy Sipowitz kicked butt!
But the cops I know are some piece of work...
With Black on Black crime at it's worse!
I can bet you all the cops will verse!
It serve's them right they'll say...
But until they give up the right to claim!
Trust between real cops and the main!
Will never, never change!
That's why we love our TV cops.

'Waiting for the Tube'

I was waiting for the tube the other day
And thought to myself, isn't this fun!
Now I will take a journey where!
Hardly anyone smiles or speaks!
Where it's hard to breathe because the air is so thin...
A journey where I might be delayed for some time,
Because there's a fault with the trains or with the lines!
Isn't this fun I thought!
To take a journey along a road of track,
Where vermin live and breed!
And germs spread from others to me.
Where it takes 45 minutes,
From Kilburn Park to Harrow Weald!
Isn't this fun I thought while waiting for the tube last week?

'Teflon'

Pulled to the left!
And pulled to the right!
Stuffed in an envelope!
Left out of sight!
Stuck in a rout!
Living in a box!
Nothing on TV!
This poems sucks!

Slapped in the face!
Kicked in the nuts!
Left for dead!
Nothing much!
Had a friend!
Lost a mate!
That's just typical!
Isn't that great!

Have no car!
Have no grace!
Spent my money!
In cyberspace!
Was he pushed?
Did he fall?
God only knows!
Nothing at all!

Am I right?
Are they wrong?
Pick up the pieces!
Must be Teflon!
Time to end this!
Getting bored!
Did I dream this?
Guess I'll never know!

'Weekly Schedule'

This week's schedule is an interesting one,
Monday is work I know but still has to be done.
Tuesday is not so bad;
I have to fly to Rome to sing a song.
Wednesday is cool because that's when I see you.
Thursday is hot, tell me what's not!
Friday I am back in London to finish that track.
Saturday I'll watch Liverpool kick Man U's butt!
Sunday I'll run to compete in the marathon.
A new weekly schedule arrives in my inbox!
Here we go again,
When will it stop?

'Indecision'

I believed the things they said,
That this whole world will fade away!
But it's my time, so set me free!
Isn't life just one big dream?

Indecision...
Sacrifice...
Once forbidden...
Let's make it right!
Let's do it right!

Broken wings!
But still we can fly...
These memories!
We'll leave behind!
But it's not too late!
So set us free!
What is life suppose to be?

Indecision...
Sacrifice...
Once forbidden...
Let's make it right!

So it's never too late!
So set us free!
Life is just one big dream!

‘Human’

'Empty Soul'

Slowly, Falling, Leaf!
Patient, Silent, Screams!
Stolen, Moments, Me!
I can't see the wood's for the trees!

So who knows where the Wind's will blow?
Inside this Empty Soul

Summer, winter, spring!
People, walking so free!
But Heaven's calling me!
We can't see the wood's for the trees!

And who knows when the winds will blow?
Inside this Empty Soul!

Slowly falling Leaf!
Patient, Silent, Screams!
Stolen moments me!
I can't see the wood's for the trees!

So who knows where the winds will blow?
Inside this Empty Soul!
Who knows when the Wind's will Blow?
Inside This Empty Soul!

'Free'

I'll take this world into my hands!
And shape it into a place I can live!
I guess you just don't understand!
Why don't you ever listen?

I just want to live...
I just want to be free to be who I am...
I just want to live...
I just want to be free...

Don't tell me there's something else!
Just look around and see what we've done...
Broken women and broken men!
Won't justify the reason...

And I just want to live...
I just want to be free to be who I am...
I just want to live...
I just want to be free...

'The Beautiful Ones'

Sometimes when you're looking for love..!
It finds you when you least expect it.
He or She can just be around the corner..!
But you have to be patient..!

Love is beautiful but it's the beautiful ones!
That make's it even more wonderful...
That's right the beautiful one's!
You're one...Even if you think you are not...

You see everyone seems to think they need to look,
Act or feel!
A certain way to find their Beautiful one!
But this may not be the case!

The beautiful one's I am talking about are the ones!
We never notice but do notice..!
Yes! You know what I am talking about..!
They may not dress very well or look attractive..!
But these are the one's that are truly beautiful..!

Yes maybe the Light that they shine, can't be seen..!
But if you look real close, you will see the light..!
So to all of you out there who think you are a beautiful one!
Think again, your light maybe can be seen straight away but the true Beautiful one's, their light shines much brighter!

'Hero's'

Hero's are everywhere!
Don't you think?
Sportsmen, Sportswomen!
Firemen, firewomen!

Hero's are everywhere!
Doctors, Nurses!
Policemen and Policewomen!
Hero's are everywhere!

But what is a Hero?
Are you one Am I one?
Who knows?

I know one hero!
She's alone in life and in mind!
She does not talk!
Sometimes she screams but just to be heard!
She cannot walk!
She cannot see!
But knowing she's there!
Makes us all feel!
That with this hero!
We can all believe!
That Hero's are everywhere!
Don't you think?

The Mirror

Yesterday I noticed an interesting thing...
What I saw was my reflection in the mirror...
It stopped me in my tracks and left me looking back...
Back to moment's in my life...!
Moment's good and bad...
And although I regret something's...
And I also treasure others...
I was left wondering about who I am...
But hey, that's normal right...?

Now Mirror's are a wonderful thing...
When u look into one...
You see many things...
No matter how many times you do...
You are still never satisfied with what you see...
A mirror is just a reflection of us and everything around us
but still we see fault in that. Why?
Well! Because we choose to...!
One is never happy with one's appearance...
One's Look is important...
It show's you how others see you and how you look throughout the day...
For me I rarely look into a mirror...
Why you may ask?
Well, because I don't need to look into a mirror to see just who I am or how I look...
I am confident with me no matter what...
And always will be...
I really don't worry about personal vanity,
what matters to me most in life is family...
So remember a reflection is just a reflection...
Look beyond the reflection and you will see much, much more than you can ever imagine.
And only then, that's when you will see the real you...

'When We Fail'

It stand's to reason,
When we fail to try then its goodbye!
Searching never reaching!
Got to sacrifice... this somehow!
I Try to hold on to just the simple things in life!
Sing when you're winning!
So the story goes...that's alright!

I've seen the funny side!
Spinning round and round...must you cry?
Why should we go to war?
Better close the door...this time!
And I've seen that look before!
In my mother's eyes...can't deny!
So sing when you're winning!
That's the way it goes!
Tell no lies!

So when the sun goes down!
When the moon is high!
When the rain keeps falling!
When the stars are bright!
When the wind blow's wild!
And the rain keeps falling!
It stand's to reason!
That when we fail to try!
Then it's goodbye!

'Wiseman'

Take that old man!
You know the one over there!
He doesn't do much does he?
True!
All he does is just begs people for money & food!
What is he like?
He is a pest to society!
That's what he is like!
Someone should do something about him!
What do you think?
I think so too, I think so too!

I am an old man!
I live on the street!
I've lost everything!
Now I have nothing!
No family no friend's!
I was a Wiseman once!
Now I am a Beggar man!
I fought for my country you know!
But now my country doesn't fight for me!
I am lost without a trace!
The people over there laugh and shout at me!
They wish I wasn't here!
So do I! So do I!

'My last stand'

This is my last stand!
I don't know how to feel!
I don't know what to do...I am lost!

Been told a million times!
To stand on my own two feet!
Live with the dignity of being a man!

I told myself one day!
That everything will be alright!
No need to sacrifice my very soul!

Friend's will come and go!
That's just my history!
I don't need any sympathy!
I don't need to know!

So just like a rainbow!
That comes when it pours!
On a summer's day!
That's how you know!

This is my last stand!
I don't know what to do!
I don't know what to say...Guess I am lost!

'Summer'

Sitting here all alone!
And just across the way!
I can hear two men grown!
Spat for spat!
They battle with words!
Chorus of sentences never heard!

One step forward!
Two steps back!
Here I sit within the crack!
Pollen in the air!
Kiddies with no hair!
Stuffed up nostrils!
Summer in London!
Me...I really don't care!

Spies are us!
So they say!
If that's the case!
Lovers beware!
Holland Park!
Hampstead Heath!
Every weekend becomes a feat!

I will try to enjoy the sun!
No matter how much!
My nose will run!
For here I sit all alone!
Oh dear! This is just too much!
I guess it's time for me to go home!

'Human'

Human is being!
Human is mankind!
Human are you,
Human is me!
Human knows!
That man must be free!

Human's are right,
Human's are wrong!
Human's believe,
That they belong!

Human's die!
Human's fail!
Human's always, live to tell!

Human's breed!
Human's kill!
Without ever knowing!
What is real!

Human's are Human!
What else is new!
Look into his heart!
And you will see you!

So human is being!
Human is mankind!
Here I sit writing this rhyme!
Deep in my soul!
I know its right.
That Human I may be!
But still life remains unkind!

‘Love’

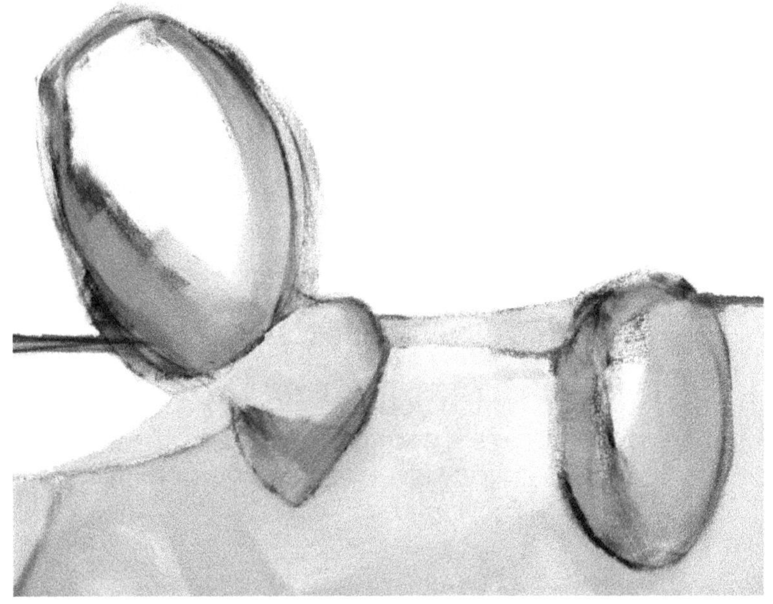

'Love'

You know when you meet someone!
You think to yourself well I hope this is the one!
He or she make's you feel great inside!
And deep inside you no longer have to hide!
When you fall in love!
Love becomes you!
When passion is all!
Love is true!

Every moment spent with him or her!
Becomes life itself!
And every moment apart!
Make's life a little bit hard!
With every touch and every kiss!
Is a moment of total bliss!
And when your eyes meet!
Your heart sometimes skip's a beat!

When you make love!
There's nothing so tender!
Because when two become one
There's nothing better!

These days, staying in love is hard!
With Life's ups and downs!
And the world around!
Love is love and should never be renounced!
Cherish love and love will cherish you!
Remember the first time it touched you!
Human's we may be!
But love is the key!
That bind's us together!
For eternity!

'First Kiss'

Her hands were shaking as they,
Reached for his!
She didn't dare tell him
She desired a kiss!
She wanted it to happen naturally!
She waited for him to reach for her!
So tenderly he held her hand!
Softly he pulled her near!
With eye's so wide!
She shook with fear!
And in that moment!
The kiss was there!

'Heaven'

Hey! Little girl!
Where do you go when things goes wrong?
With a smile you take my breath away!
I need to know...little girl!

I see you in my dreams!
And now I know I'll never be alone!
Now! That I've seen Heaven in your eyes!

Hey! Pretty Girl!
With just one touch I come alive!
When I hold you close in my arms!
It feel's so right...Pretty Girl!

And when you call out my name!
I know that my heart will never be the same!
Now! That I've seen Heaven once again!

Hey! Little girl!
Where do you go when it goes wrong?
With a smile you take my breath away!
I need your love...little girl!

I see you in my dreams!
And now I know I'll never be alone!
When you call out my name!
I know that my heart will never be the same...Again!
Now! That I've seen Heaven in your eyes!
I've seen Heaven...in your eyes!

'I Found Her'

I found you,
It was so easy!
I looked and there you were!
A vision of love in front of me!
I knew then,
I could never leave!

Give me a reason to believe!
Show me heaven if you please!
My heart now belongs to thee!
She's the one who now hold's the key!

Her eyes pierce deep through me!
Hey smile make's me happy!
Her touch leave's me thinking!
Her laugh keeps me guessing!

I found her,
It was easy!
Now my heart breathes more freely!
A vision of love she blinds me!
I know now,
I could never leave!

'It's you'

I was left outside!
Lived amongst the shadows!
What a waste of time!
Can't you see my halo?

Yes I did you wrong!
I made mistakes I know!
Can't turn back the time!
Deep inside I think you know!

Now I realise!
When a heart is on the line!
You just got to fight!
For everything that matters!

And it's you!
It's always been you!
Yes it's true!
It always was you!

'Meant To Be'

I Say To You...
Take the Sunlight from My Eyes!
Take Away All the Beauty,
All the Lies!
I Can't Hear...Can You Say Three Little Words?
My Sins and Fears!
I'm The One They Said Would Burn!

This Thing in Me,
It Needs To Be!
This Thing I Feel...Is Meant...to be!

They Don't Know,
What It Feels Like To Burn!
Take what's mine,
All the Wonders in the World!
My Hopes and Dreams!
Are Like Candles in the Wind!
Now I Believe,
This Was Always Destiny!

This Thing in Me!
It Need's To Be!
This Thing I Feel!
Was Meant...To Be!

'That Girl'

There's this girl right!
Wow! What a female!
Every time I see her!
I lose it a little!

She doesn't even know I am alive!
I wish she did!
Her hair is long!
Her skin is pure!
But somehow I know she isn't!

Her body looks firm!
Her legs in that skirt make's me yearn!
God I wish she was mine!
But oh look, here comes her guy!

He drive's a Black BMW!
I don't even drive!
What chance do I have to have what he has?

I know I shouldn't covet someone else's girl!
But if it work's in the movies why can't it work for me?
Got to stop watching that bloody MTV!

It's best I find someone who loves me for me.
But still I wish it was her!
Urban dreamer, wow that girl is so sexy!

'Sleep'

See her falling!
Just a picture!
With no meaning!
Don't cry no more!
Don't close the door!
Wipe away your tears!
Lady!

She once told me!
Memories!
With her beauty!
She tempts me in!
Close your eyes!
Go to sleep!
I'll stroke your hair!
So sleep for me!
Sleep for me!

'The One'

To me you are like air!
Without you I couldn't breathe!
Your eyes are embedded in my soul!
When you are near!
I can hear every beat of your heart!
And with every moment that passes!
Your smile brightens my day, and warms my nights!
So come to me my love!
Be the one to love me!
Be the one I want to marry!
My dearest one you are my life!

'Stay'

Last night I dreamt I was the apple!
The apple in your eyes!
Like a rose you held me close!
And in the summer sun!
We danced until the moon shone above!
You surrendered to my heart!

Just to watch you comb your hair!
Sends shivers down my spine!
Your reflection make's me smile!
The beauty of your face!
Eases my mind in these scoundrel days!
I know these words could not express!

So won't you please stay?
Just a little longer!
I know love's fate!
Will save me once again!
Won't you please stay?
Just a little longer!
I knew one day!
I'd find love once again!

'Left of Centre'

There's a place I knew in you!
Where my heart once stood!
Every day was heaven sent!
Cherished moment's spent with you!
Like a bird love flew away!
Just like a storm it ended!
These are the days of my life!
No more beginnings!

There's a place deep in my mind!
Memories of you!
Another road in which I find!
Myself walking through!
Like a bird you flew away!
Just like a storm we ended!
These are the days of our lives!
No more pretending!

I've been through the wind and rain!
I've been lost without a trace!
Locked in a dungeon far away!
Left of centre...Once again!

'A Love Unknown'

I knew her for just a short while!
She told me that I shouldn't be so wild!
I asked her if she knew...
All that she would do!
But still inside I felt like a child!

Meeting once was never enough!
Because now she hate's me with all her guts!
We talked with love within our hearts!
But now she looks through me like a plain of glass!
Broken inside I will always be!
Not knowing what her love could have been!
So now she writes Blogs to be seen!
To make me out like an has been!

I think of her everyday!
Because deep inside I know she still cares!
We said things that we regret!
And now she spies on me...
Like a science project!
Will we ever speak again!
I don't know!
But what I do know!
Is that she foretold..!
That I am in hell...
And I don't even know...
But my love for her
remains unknown!

'A Love Returned'

I saw her on the tube!
It had been year or two since we last met!
I tapped her shoulder!
And called out her name!
She turned and with a broad smile!
She replied, Mark Oh my!
We hugged and kissed!
How beautiful was still she!
Her eyes pierced through me!
Her hair smelt lovely!
My heart skipped a beat!
The love I once cherished!
Had returned to me!

Finally I told her!
Just how I felt about her!
All those years ago!
Surprised she was but happy I know!
Then it was time for her to go!
So I gave her my card to make sure!
I blew her a kiss!
And said goodbye once more!
Now we talk all the time!
And she has become,
The best thing in my life!
The girl I loved from a distance!
Keep's me safe and wise!
One day I hoped she would be!
A love Returned...to me!

'Much Too Late'

Seven days,
Without you by my side!
The warning signs,
I just didn't heed them this time!
I've waited too long,
And now my best friend is gone!

'It's much too late' to say goodbye!
I wish I could turn back the hands of time!
'It's much too late' to make it right!
Time won't you save me somehow!

We're two of a kind!
I rehearsed the word's I wanted to say!
No more making plans!
Got to find a way to make you stay!

Is it so wrong?
Living this aching moment!
I've waited too long!
And now my best friend is gone!

'Gone For Good'

Too many time's I said, forever!
Too many time's I watched it fail...
Could it be that I'm just so restless?
Could it be that I'm just so scared?

Now looking back I see no reason...
No reason for me to feel ashamed!
Love is to understand
It's just an empty feeling in my head...!

She's, gone forever...
She's gone for good!
Once more alone!
Misunderstood!

Sleepless nights and feeling lonely...
All I do is watch the skies!
Could it be that I'm just so stupid?
Could it be that I'm a fool?

Looking back I see no reason...
No reason to play this game!
Because love is understanding,
I've got no one but myself to blame!

That's why she's gone forever...
She's gone for good!
Once more the fool!
Misunderstood!

'Don't Want To Know'

Everybody wants to know!
But I'll never tell them so!
So keep your distance!
From my door!
'Coz, I don't want to know!
The word's you say don't mean a thing!
Take your keys take back this ring!
So keep your distance from my door!
Because I don't want to know!
I don't want to know!

I've been up and down this street!
I've been wondering what to eat!
Picture postcards memories,
I tell you that's not for me!
Palpitations in my head!
Was it something that you said?
So keep your distance from my door!
'Coz, I don't want to know!
I said I don't want to know!

Severed from my history!
It was never chemistry!
So keep your distance from my door!
'Coz, I don't want to know!
I don't want to know...
I don't want to know...

'Without you'

What am I to make of this?
What am I to say?
I lift my head from uneasy pillows!
Just to find you not there!

Every morning it's something different!
I can't believe!
What she said!
Homer Simpson makes my evenings!
I guess it's time to pray!

Bright light shines through my window!
But I still can't see!
Just why you had to leave me!
Hanging on a string!

Picking up the pieces slowly!
Learning how to breathe again!
I put on some good soul music!
Just to ease the pain!

Can't you hear me calling?
From far away I'm shouting!
I'll crawl on my knees to find you!
I just can't stand another day without you!

So what am I to make of this?
What am I to say?
When Homer Simpson makes my evenings
I guess it's time I prayed...

'I Don't Want To Be'

An evening star burns through my window!
The dusty road begins to break!
I've been listening to your thoughts all night!
The waking moment never changes!

Foreign skies made me surrender!
A passive summer made it right!
I took a hold of something different to mind!
A simple feeling lost with time!
And I say!

I don't want to be!
I don't want to be the one you say goodbye to babe!
I don't want to live!
I don't want to live my life without you babe!

I'm reaching out to find some reason!
Now won't you justify your crime!
And did I hear you say, you needed me tonight?
Because Baby I can read the signs!
Now you say!

I don't want to be!
I don't want to be the one you say goodbye to babe!
I don't want to live!
I don't want to live my life without you babe!

MARK.J.STEVENS

Simple Man...
Don't you run away!
Keep your head held high
Don't you ever stray!
This Simple Man...
With these eyes so bright!
Don't you fall away!
Don't you ever stray!

This book is dedicated to Diane Williamson 1968-2005

RIP

MJ Stevens

Special thanks to...

Jitka Jemelkova, Steve Sailsman, Laura Romero, Samantha Underdown, Lourdes Salcedo-Tavira, Zuzana Stalmachova and Kristiina Jadal

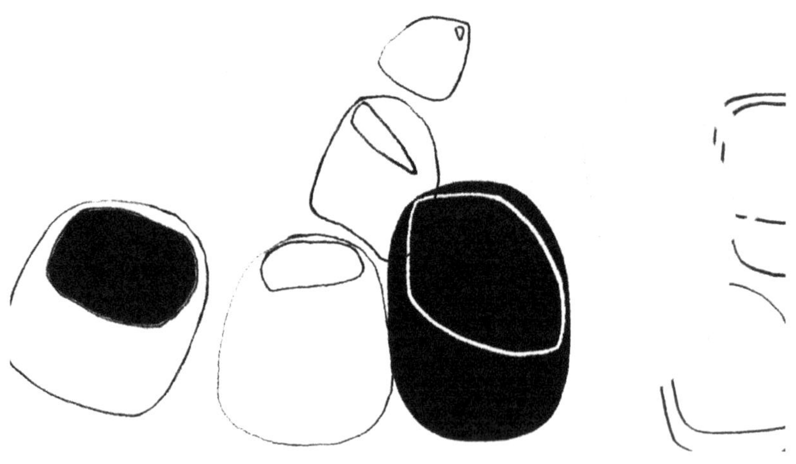

ISBN 978-1-4478-2003-1
90000
9 781447 820031

www.ingramcontent.com/pod-product-compliance
Ingram Content Group UK Ltd.
Pitfield, Milton Keynes, MK11 3LW, UK
UKHW050614260726
13967UKWH00008B/2852

9 781447 820031